Pebble® Plus

Animal Kingdom Questions and Answers

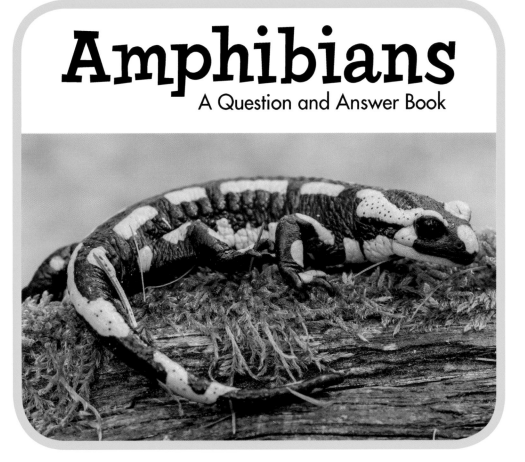
Amphibians
A Question and Answer Book

by Isabel Martin

Consulting Editor: Gail Saunders-Smith, PhD

CAPSTONE PRESS
a capstone imprint

T0061177

Pebble Plus is published by Capstone Press,
1710 Roe Crest Drive, North Mankato, Minnesota 56003
www.capstonepub.com

Copyright © 2015 by Capstone Press, a Capstone imprint. All rights reserved. No part of this publication may be reproduced in whole or in part, or stored in a retrieval system, or transmitted in any form or by any means, electronic, mechanical, photocopying, recording, or otherwise, without written permission of the publisher.

Library of Congress Cataloging-in-Publication Data
Martin, Isabel, 1977–
    Amphibians : a question and answer book / by Isabel Martin.
        pages cm. — (Pebble plus. Animal kingdom questions and answers)
    Includes bibliographical references and index.
    Summary: "Simple text and colorful images illustrate types of amphibians, including common characteristics, diet, and life cycle"—Provided by publisher.
    Audience: Ages 4–8.
    Audience: Grades K–3.
    ISBN 978-1-4914-0562-8 (library binding) — ISBN 978-1-4914-0630-4 (paperback) — ISBN 978-1-4914-0596-3 (eBook PDF)
    1. Amphibians—Juvenile literature. I. Title.
    QL644.2.M3153 2015
    597.8—dc23   2013050338

Editorial Credits
Nikki Bruno Clapper, editor; Cynthia Akiyoshi, designer; Kelly Garvin, media researcher;
Katy LaVigne, production specialist

Photo Credits
Dreamstime/Alptraum, cover, back cover; Minden Pictures: Michael Durham, 5, Michael & Patricia Fogden, 7, Thomas Marent, 19; Shutterstock: Alin Brotea, 11, Dirk Ercken, 15, 21, Joe Farah, 9, Marek R. Swadzba, 1, Paul Broadbent, 17; Superstock/F.Rauschenbach/F1 OLINE, 13

Note to Parents and Teachers

The Animal Kingdom Questions and Answers set supports national curriculum standards for science related to the diversity of living things. This book describes and illustrates the characteristics of amphibians. The images support early readers in understanding the text. The repetition of words and phrases helps early readers learn new words. This book also introduces early readers to subject-specific vocabulary words, which are defined in the Glossary section. Early readers may need assistance to read some words and to use the Table of Contents, Glossary, Read More, Internet Sites, Critical Thinking Using the Common Core, and Index sections of the book.

Printed in the United States   5498

Table of Contents

Meet the Amphibians

Hop, hop! A frog jumps.
Frogs, toads, and newts
are called amphibians.
These animals come in many
shapes, colors, and sizes.

Pacific tree frog

Do Amphibians Have Backbones?

Yes, amphibians have backbones.

Caecilians are very bendy.

Their backbones have lots of

tiny bones called vertebrae.

Say it like this:

caecilians

(si-SIL-yuhnz)

caecilian

Are Amphibians Warm-Blooded or Cold-Blooded?

Amphibians are cold-blooded.

Their body temperatures change

with their surroundings.

Couch's spadefoot toad

What Type of Body Covering Do Amphibians Have?

Amphibians have smooth, moist skin. Sometimes they outgrow their skin, and it peels off. This is called molting.

salamander

How Do Amphibians Eat?

Amphibians eat worms, insects, and other small animals.

Most amphibians sit still and snatch prey that passes by.

pool frog

Where Do Amphibians Live?

Amphibians live in water and on land.

Many live near ponds or in forests.

Some amphibians can live in dry

places such as deserts.

poison dart frog

How Do Amphibians Have Young?

Amphibians lay eggs in water. The eggs have soft skin that feels like jelly. Baby toads and frogs are called tadpoles.

toad tadpoles

Do Amphibians Care for Their Young?

Some amphibians care for their young for a short time. Many amphibians guard their eggs until they hatch.

eggs

midwife toad

What Is a Cool Fact About Amphibians?

Amphibians can get air in three ways. Baby amphibians get air underwater with gills. Adults breathe with lungs. They also get air through their skin.

crested newt

gills

21

Glossary

adult—an animal that is fully grown

caecilian—a wormlike amphibian with no legs

cold-blooded—having a body temperature that changes with the surrounding temperature

gill—a body part on the side of a fish or a young amphibian; gills are used to take air into the body

hatch—to break out of an egg

lung—a large body part inside the chest; lungs are used for breathing

moist—a little bit wet

molt—to shed an outer layer of skin

newt—a small amphibian with short legs and a long tail

tadpole—the stage of a frog's or toad's growth between the egg and adult stages; tadpoles live in water

temperature—the measure of how hot or cold something is

vertebra—one of the small bones that make up a backbone

Read More

Bredeson, Carmen. *Fun Facts About Salamanders!* I Like Reptiles and Amphibians! Berkeley Heights, N.J.: Enslow, 2008.

Guiberson, Brenda Z. *Frog Song.* New York: Henry Holt, 2012.

Harris, Tim. *Amphibians.* Slimy, Scaly, Deadly Reptiles and Amphibians. New York: Gareth Stevens, 2010.

Internet Sites

FactHound offers a safe, fun way to find Internet sites related to this book. All of the sites on FactHound have been researched by our staff.

Here's all you do:
Visit www.facthound.com
Type in this code: 9781491405628

 Super-cool stuff! Check out projects, games and lots more at www.capstonekids.com

Critical Thinking Using the Common Core

1. How do amphibians take care of their eggs? (Key Ideas and Details)

2. What is a caecilian? How are caecilians different from other amphibians? (Craft and Structure)

Index

Word Count: 174
Grade: 1
Early-Intervention Level: 16